小人国的于子中

The Story of John Yoo

-2-

故事、插画：潘楚珩

written and illustrated by Ellen Pan

Book design by Ellen Pan

ISBN 978-1-959128-72-4 (paperback)

www.lithousepublishing.com

前言

  我从三岁八个月开始读了第一本中文书，到现在有将近十五年了。这些年我读过很多中英文书，自己也陆续写过一些中英文的绘本书，在这个过程中获得了极大的乐趣。我看到很多人觉得中文很难学，于是萌生了一个想法：我想写一本中文的启蒙绘本，帮助学生用很短的时间学会一些常用字，读一些简单的书，使学习中文变得有趣，令初学者也能体会到读中文书的成就感。于是我写了这一系列关于于子中的故事。《小人国的于子中》第一册和第二册一共用到了两百个不同的汉字。这两百个汉字是现代汉语口最常用到的，累计使用频率超过百分之五十五。如果学生一天学会十个汉字，那么二十天就可以读这两本书了。后面随着故事发展，每一本都会增加一些常用字。这个系列的故事读完，就能学会几百个常用字，读中文书就会变得简单多了。希望家长和孩子们能够喜欢于子中的故事。

潘楚珩

二零二四年六月

Not only did Yicheng miss his chance at going to Liliput last time, but he also became very very small. He was not happy about this at all.

nà yī rì fāng yǐ chéng méi néng qù xiǎo rén guó, hái dāng le yì huí xiǎo bù
那一日方以成没能去小人国，还当了一回小不
diǎn er tā hěn bù kāi xīn
点儿，他很不开心。

Yicheng was a general in Ruyi's army and had a lot of power. But he still wanted to get a more important position in the future. Actually, it'd be even better if he became a minister.

他本来是如意国的一员大将，身在高位，很有实力。不过，他现在当着一等大将军，还想着新一任最好能当上相国。

Yicheng wondered if he could become Liliput's ruler and have their people make things for him. That would make his life much better.

fāng yǐ chéng xiǎng　rú guǒ néng dāng shàng xiǎo rén guó de yì guó zhī zhǔ　lì
方 以 成 想，如 果 能 当 上 小 人 国 的 一 国 之 主，利
yòng xiǎo rén guó wèi tā zhì zuò dōng xi　kě néng yǐ hòu jiù yǒu jī huì dāng shàng xiāng
用 小 人 国 为 他 制 作 东 西，可 能 以 后 就 有 机 会 当 上 相
guó
国。

But he couldn't go to John's home. Who knew what could happen if he got caught a second time? Suddenly, Yicheng was reminded of the Princess of Ruyi.

但是他又不能去于子中的家。下次被于子中看见，还不知道会发生什么事。这时他想起了如意国的公主。

She never left her palace, but she knew everything.
Well-read, beautiful, and kind—what a wonderful lady!

公主天天都在家不出门，可海内外的事她无所不知，她有文化，人又美，性情也好。

Yicheng decided that he would visit her tomorrow and ask if she had any ideas.

见公主时该送什么

fāng yǐ chéng xiǎng yào míng tiān tè yì qù kàn kan gōng zhǔ wèn wen tā yǒu méi
方以成想要明天特意去看看公主，问问她有没
shén shí me hǎo shǐ de zhǔ yì
有什么好使的主意。

The next day, Yicheng greeted the Princess with gifts from his hometown and let her know his requests.

方以成手上提了本地物产，到公主的家里来看她，并说明了来意。公主果然什么都知道。

The Princess really did know everything! " John Yoo is indeed very small now, but he used to be normal," she said.

tā shuō 　　　 yú zǐ zhōng xiàn zài shì hěn xiǎo 　　 bú guò 　 xiān qián tā shì zhèng
她说：" 于子中现在是很小，不过，先前他是正
cháng de
常的。

His family had all passed away, and he was rarely happy. His only wish was to live a better life.

他家里的亲人都已经去世了。他一度过得很不好，只想有一日能成家立业。

One day two years ago, John found an old man from Liliput in his little farm.

liǎng nián qián de yì tiān   yú zǐ zhōng qù dì lǐ   fā xiàn le yī cè xǎo rén guó
两年前的一天，于子中去地里，发现了一个小人国
de lǎo zhě
的老者。

He gave the old man his own food. The man thought John was very polite and kind, so he taught him Liliput's spells.

于子中把自己的果子给了老者。

The man thought John was very polite and kind, so he taught him Liliput's spells.

好人！

这位老者看到于子中很斯文，心地也很好，就教给了他《小人国经》与《大人国经》。"

"However," the princess said, "after he uses the Miniput chant, he can grow back to his original size in a month—but this only works ten times. After that, he stays small. Now, he needs to live on his own for three years before someone from Liliput takes him there."

"不过，"公主又说道："《小人国经》用过以后，一个月内可以重新回到原来的身高。用过十次以后，身体就回不去原来的大小了。这时于子中要自己生活，还不能去小人国，第三年会有人来到他家，和他一起去小人国。"

"I believe that John hasn't been to Liliput, and you won't be able to either." The Princess rose: "Ruyi and Liliput are friendly countries towards each other. Their representatives visit us every year; we have no reason to make war with them."

"所以我相信他是没有去过小人国的，你也去不了。他说的是对的。"公主立起身，高声对方以成说："小人国政通人和，与我们也有合作。他们年年有代表来我国，并没有对不起我们的地方。我们不应向他们开战。"

Yicheng couldn't think of a good response off the top of his head, so he left defeated.

huà shuō dào zhè er fāng yǐ chéng yì shí jiān bù zhī dào yīng shuō shén me
话说到这儿，方以成一时间不知道应说什么，
zhǐ hǎo qǐ shēn huí jiā
只好起身回家。

Meanwhile, John had no idea about this conversation, but everything the Princess said was completely true.

于子中不知道方以成这头的行动。不过公主所说的他的事，都是实情。

In the first year that John learned the Liliput spells, he could change between being small and normal-sized.

他学会《小人国经》的头一年，可以当一个很小的人，也能作为正常人生活。《小人国经》用过一个月以后，他能回到原来的大小。但是用过十次以后，他就再也回不去了。

His life became much better this way.

He planted crops when he was a normal person, and didn't eat much when he was small.

可大可小的时候，于子中的生活好多了。

正常人大小的时候他就及时去种地，其他时间他用的东西也不多，这样他的生活已经很好了。

At first, he stayed home when he was small, so nobody saw. After he became small forever, people began to notice. This was also when Yicheng heard about John.

开头他只有在家的时候是小个子，大家没有看到。后来，由于他回不去正常人的大小，大家就都发现了。方以成就是这时知道的。

What John didn't know was that Yicheng had been thinking about this day and night. Eventually, he got an idea: "If I can't have Liliput, at least I can have their spells! That way, no one can tell me 'no' ever again!"

fāng yǐ chéng tiān tiān zài jiā xiǎng zhè shì hòu lái tā xiǎng bù néng qù xiǎo
方以成天天在家想这事，后来他想："不能去小
rén guó yào shì yǒu xiǎo rén guó jīng huò dà rén guó jīng yě xíng a
人国，要是有《小人国经》或《大人国经》也行啊!
yǒu le tā men cǐ dì jiù méi yǒu rén néng duì wǒ shuō bù
有了它们，此地就没有人能对我说'不'!"

This is a series of entertaining books... and a very special one. The second story of John Yoo is written with today's two hundred most commonly used Chinese characters. If you want to read the first two stories as a beginner to Chinese, all you have to do is learn ten characters a day—twenty days in total. These two hundred characters constitute, in frequency, over 55% of all characters that are used in the Chinese language, so they will be integral to all Chinese reading in the future. As we move along the series, every book will use an additional one hundred characters; I hope that you can enjoy the humor, fun, and surprising simplicity of the Chinese language as you continue learning through the stories of John Yoo.

这是一系列很特别也很有趣的书。每本书在前一本的基础上增加一百个使用频率最高的生字。如果一位初学者想学会读这两本书，那么每天认识十个字，只需要二十天就可以了。这两百个字在汉字中的累计使用频率超过百分之五十五，所以在未来的阅读中，它们也将是非常有用的。后续的故事集中，每一册都会增加一百个常用字。希望读者在学习的过程中能够感到轻松又有趣。愿你们喜欢于子中的故事。

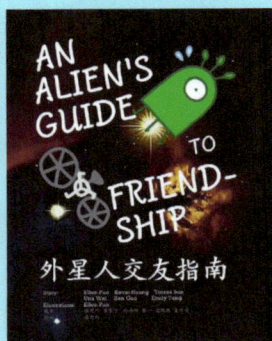

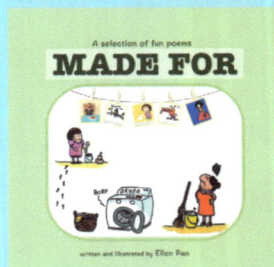

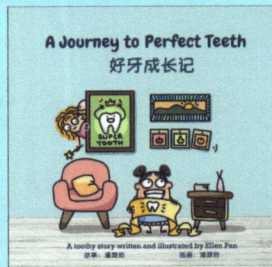

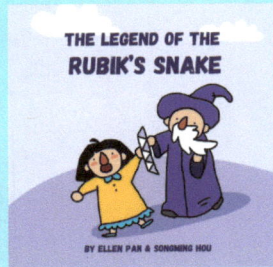

Ellen Pan is a writer and illustrator who has authored children's books in English, Chinese, and French. She is studying Applied Math and Visual Art at Harvard College.

Above are some other books by Ellen Pan.

潘楚珩用英文、中文、法语创作儿童书并绘制插画。她现在正在哈佛大学学习应用数学和视觉艺术专业。以上是她的其他一些作品。

www.ingramcontent.com/pod-product-compliance
Lightning Source LLC
Chambersburg PA
CBHW042058040426
42447CB00003B/269